FRAGMENTS OBSERVED:
Lessons Learned on Patrol

Carrie Dalby

Copyright ©2026 Carrie Dalby Cox

All rights reserved. No part of this publication may be reproduced, distributed, or transmitted in any form or by any means, including photocopying, recording, or other electronic or mechanical methods, without the prior written permission of the publisher, except in the case of brief quotations embodied in reviews and certain other noncommercial uses permitted by copyright law.
For permission requests, please contact the publisher.

Book designed and published by Olive Kent Publishing, Mobile, Alabama

Original watercolor on the cover by Jacqueline Parks

Title and chapter fonts: Yataghan—Bold
Story text: Garamond

carriedalby.com

*For all the Mobile Police Department squads I've
ridden with,
especially my hosting officers,
thank you for sharing your patrol with me.*

Table of Contents

Introduction

1. Roll Call   13
2. Community is Key   30
3. Kindness Goes a Long Way   67
4. Embrace Humor   90
5. Check Off   117

Acknowledgments   128

For More Information   131

About the Author

Introduction

"Because we fail to listen to each other's stories we are becoming a fragmented human race."
–Madeleine L'Engle

On February 28, 2024, I walked into a police station and haven't been the same since. A quest for three key items of historic information from the Mobile Police Department (MPD) turned into a multi-year journey of education, introspection, and growth.

The rabbit hole that led to me racking up 156 hours of patrol time with MPD (as of the end of 2025) started when I sought to finalize details in my manuscript for *Loyalty: Washington Square Secrets 3*. I had searched my usual haunting grounds of local libraries, archives, and museums for the better part of a year before deciding I should reach out directly to the Mobile Police Department. As a believer that everything happens for a reason, I know the inspiration came at the right time. I wrote my questions about the uniforms, gear, and possible patrol vehicles from 1920 in a Facebook message to the MPD page and gave them permission to pass my contact information to someone that might be able to help. An hour later, Captain Billie Rowland, acting MPD historian, emailed me saying he could probably answer my questions. I immediately set up an appointment to visit him.

What I found two days later when I walked into the precinct he commanded wasn't a station full of thugs sitting around in handcuffs that Hollywood throws at us nor the chaos of noise and people from my one previous experience at MPD headquarters when I had gone to the headquarters building in the late 1990s to give a statement to a detective about an armed robbery. My mother and I witnessed the suspect—a man with a purse—run from the parking lot of a store to the back of the building and jump into a waiting car as I drove into the shopping center. After spotting a crying woman with several people trying to comfort her, we turned around and followed the getaway car until they stopped at a gas station a few miles away. After seeing where they went, we returned to the scene to report what we saw to the responding police officer.

The precinct foyer that winter morning was clean and functional, the front desk staff polite. Though I went in hoping the meeting would give me answers, I was shielded behind a layer of skepticism, having been treated indifferently before when seeking research due to the fact that I am a novelist, not a "real writer" according to some people.

When I was escorted through the security door separating the foyer from the back, it was eerily quiet in the hallway of mostly closed doors. If I had to imagine walking a plank, it would have felt like that inaugural excursion to the precinct commander's office. I was even slightly dizzy with nerves, adding to the feeling of being on a ship as the fluorescent lights gleamed off the shiny floor. But what I saw when I stepped into the open door of Captain Rowland's office put me at ease. There were bookcases filled with nonfiction titles across multiple interests alongside action figures, assorted mementos, and photographs. It was homey and the goateed captain turned out to be as welcoming as his office.

After a brief introduction, I settled in a chair across from the precinct commander at the long edge of his L-shaped desk, which had several piles of books and folders. The short end of the desk housed two large screens and other computer items. I thanked him for seeing me, explained my status as a historical fiction author and reiterated the questions from my original note.

Captain Rowland addressed my questions, showing me department photographs and letters from the archives that supported the information while I recorded items of interest in my notebook. Then he enthusiastically used one of his computer screens to skim through the MPD history slideshow he uses to teach the recruits at the Police Academy, giving me a crash course in their history. Not only did my skepticism leave after seeing that a police captain with over thirty years' experience took my questions seriously, I was also amazed at how much information was not easily accessible to the public, especially since the Police Museum had closed a few years previously. When Captain Rowland shared that he was almost done compiling a manuscript chronicling the Mobile Police Department's history, I promised to assist him in seeing it to publication because an MPD history book would benefit families, researchers, and the whole community.

In the months that followed, e-mails were exchanged as clarifying questions came to the surface during my subsequent editorial rounds on the novel. There were also errands I volunteered to go on to assist Captain Rowland with MPD research when he couldn't get away from his office, plus local history books I found on my ramblings that I shared with him. If I happened across mentions of the police department while digging into research for my next novel, I shared them with him.

After a year of collaborative researching, editing, and formatting, *Unbroken Service: A History of the Mobile Police Department* by Billie L. Rowland was published in May 2025. Now all those hard-to-find MPD facts are available for everyone, no trip to the precinct commander's office needed. In kind, Captain Rowland read my manuscripts for *Loyalty: Washington Square Secrets 3* and *Betrayal: Washington Square Secrets 4* before they were published to check for MPD accuracy, the ultimate quality inspection for historical fiction.

Amid my research, I thought it would be good to have a solid knowledge base about the local police today. It would assist me in deciding which historic details would be best to share in my novels so I could showcase what had changed or stayed the same. To further my understanding without having to bother Captain Rowland with all my questions, I started a ten-week course offered by MPD called the Citizens Police Academy in the spring of 2024. The weekly classes covered the structure of the police department including the different units and the resources available to the community. And there were field trips and the opportunity to do ride-alongs in the precincts of your choice.

"Do a ride-along," the lieutenant said that first night of class, "and see first-hand how the officers work."

With his added words of "You'll probably take someone to jail and see the sally port," the sally port (the secured garage entry to the jail for those under arrest) became, in my mind, the symbol of the ultimate ride-along experience.

We were told to do at least one ride during the course, even if it was only for a couple of hours. I completed three twelve-hour patrols while in the Citizens Police Academy without seeing an arrest. Since graduating in July 2024, I've been an active member of the Mobile Citizens Police Academy Alumni Association, working volunteer hours at events to support MPD through service and fundraising efforts. I did a fourth ride in the fall of that year, but still didn't even witness an arrest, which was an anomaly by all accounts.

In April 2025, I returned to ride-alongs, doing one a month through the end of the year. Family and friends jokingly said I was going to keep riding until I got to the sally port. An acquaintance with one of the local fire departments labeled me a "white cloud," someone who causes calm shifts because nothing happens around them. Playing off their teasing, I cheekily updated my hours on patrol followed by "still no sally port" when I posted about my ride on social media. The track record of non-arrest hours became a badge of oddness that only kept increasing.

But it was more than that.

I shared a monthly "Riding with the Mobile Police Department" article on my "Fragments Observed" blog beginning in June 2025 to highlight what MPD officers deal with in a typical twelve-hour shift. After drafting my fifth article, I realized I was leaving more unsaid than I was sharing. I saw the city of Mobile, its inhabitants, and those sworn to protect it in a new light. The more I witnessed, the more I changed. Seeing what goes on outside my small social bubble enhanced my outlook on life with each patrol hour. I wanted to explore those topics, but the 500-800 words in my online articles didn't allow the space to do so.

It was time to take my thoughts to book format.

What you will find here is a narrative showcasing fragments of what I have seen, wisdom learned, and how I've matured as a result of riding with Mobile's finest. Out of respect for the privacy of the victims, subjects, and officers, it isn't comprehensive. My hosting officers were male, female, Hispanic, Black, White, Native American, and Middle Eastern, reflecting the diversity of the Port City that they serve. Rather than calling out a person's looks and other possible identifying details, I purposely kept the narrative sparser than my fiction as another layer of confidentiality.

In many ways, this book is one of the hardest things I have written and certainly the most difficult to commit to publishing. On these pages, I am not able to hide behind a fictional narrator or imagined events. This is my voice, my soul, amid real happenings in an open letter to the Mobile Police Department to thank them for helping me remember what is important in life: community, kindness, and humor.

1. Roll Call

"A great attitude is not the result of
success; success is the result of a great attitude."
– Earl Nightingale

When doing a ride with the Mobile Police Department, the civilian must report to the approved precinct at the start of roll call for the shift, which varies by station. Walking into a patrol squad's roll call for the first time at all the precincts was awkward for this introvert, but entering my very first roll call in a precinct I had never visited was "first day at school in a new town in the middle of the year" level anxiety. I parked about ten minutes early. Taking stock of the officers sitting in their vehicles, I was unsure if they were closing out their day or getting ready to report for their last shift on a long holiday weekend of night patrol. Since I had arrived outside of the station's office hours, I needed a police officer to escort me inside. Choosing the nearest white Chevy Tahoe with blue and black Mobile Police Department detailing, I exhaled a cleansing breath, and walked over.

I purposely kept my empty hands at my sides when nerves had me wanting to shove them into my pockets. Why empty and visible? Officers are taught that hands kill. If you can't see a person's hands, you don't know what type of weapon they might be holding. "Show me your hands!" and "Keep your hands where I can see them!" are their go-to command phrases for a reason.

When I was about two feet away from the Tahoe, the officer lowered the passenger window.

I identified myself as being from the Citizens Academy, saying I was scheduled to ride the night shift.

"You're early," the officer stated without so much as a smile. "Go sit in your vehicle. I'll signal when it's time to go in."

Brusk, but informative. I returned to my car and waited, glad to have my initial contact over, even if it wasn't as friendly as my previous encounters with Captain Rowland or the staff at the Police Academy.

Several minutes later, the officer exited his Tahoe and motioned to me. I fumbled with the tote bag housing my metal water bottle, snacks, notebook, and purse, caught up with him at the precinct's door, and followed him through what felt like a maze of hallways. He entered a large room that had multiple rows of tables with seating for several people in each row facing the front, where another table was positioned in the center with a couple of cushioned chairs facing the other tables.

He gave a broad wave to the front rows. "Sit there."

The officer kept walking to the back of the room. I chose a seat on the second row and tried not to fidget under the weight of unease permeating the space. Yes, I was nervous, but the tension was coming from without, not within. Rather than lessen as the officers trickled in, my level of agitation grew. Half a dozen officers ranging in age from their early twenties to forties trudged by like they were entering Mordor. They all went to the back rows. Not wanting to turn and stare, I was left watching the officers who were still arriving. More funeral faces with only a few words spoken among the officers in the back. It reminded me of a job I had where I could tell if a certain assistant manager was the manager on duty for the shift based on the negative vibes in the air when I walked into the building. And those shifts weren't pleasant.

Waiting for roll call to begin, I fought the urge to shrink in my chair to hide from the sensation of unease, but it's difficult to hide when you're six-feet tall. Plus I knew they were already aware of my presence by the wide berth they were giving me. I started rethinking the paperwork I had already turned in to do two more rides. Was reporting to police work always this dreadful? I was weighing the emotional strain of wading through the turmoil just to get more hours of observation. Though seeing all aspects of a patrol officer's job was what I was after during that phase of research, I was ready to walk out.

Then an officer strutted in with a huge grin and a bright demeanor that cut through the gloomy atmosphere as he made his way to the back. At least one person groaned in annoyance while other officers murmured complaints. But I clasped a ray of hope from the light he brought into the room.

The squad leadership took their seats in the front, facing the rest of us. I can't remember if it was a lieutenant or sergeant running things (I wasn't adept at reading rank symbols back then) but he sounded tired. Towards the end of the meeting consisting of a few announcements, he acknowledged my presence then said, "Now who are you going to ride with...." He barked a last name.

"I had the last ride-along," a voice replied from behind me.

Another name.

"I had a recruit last week."

And then a third name, and another gruff excuse.

A final name was said, no questioning in the squad leader's voice. Then he glanced my way and told me the officer's name I would be with, followed by, "He's the one that doesn't want to look at you."

I wasn't offended by any of it, though I easily could have been. After a month in the academy listening to different stories, I knew enough about the stresses of the job, as well as general sociology and psychology, to recognize the officers had an underlining level of fatigue, not to mention unknown-(but felt)-to-me undercurrents going on within the squad. In addition, the Citizens Academy and Police Academy were large groups with a lot of people doing rides that month, which interrupts the patrol officers' regular rhythms. And I never forget that the officers also have their own lives with personal stress. They have family, relationships, troubles, and triumphs in their life outside of patrol time. Every officer I've met is human in all the unique ways that make this world interesting.

When we reached his Tahoe, I stood by while the assigned officer cleared the passenger seat for me. Once we were both inside, he apologized for the way things had started in the roll call room and introduced himself.

Since that first ride, I tell the officers I'm with that I am there to observe and try to be as unobtrusive as possible—that I'll be as quiet or as talkative as they prefer. Often they'll respond by saying, "It's your time, ask whatever you want" or something similar. Several times, they've asked me questions, usually about my books and writing. I'm completely open with the fact that the main reason I started riding was to observe their mannerisms and interactions, which helps me write realistic characters.

One of the most surprising questions I got was whether the Citizens Academy had held their range day yet. We had, so the officer asked me how good of a shot I was. My reply was showing him a picture of my target. He nodded his approval.

The most popular question before I was a member of the Mobile Citizens Police Academy Alumni Association (MCPAAA) was what my opinion of the police was. I never sought out police movies, shows, or books like some people do. In my head, the main police officer types were those who became officers to help people, those who joined the Police Academy because they want to get the bad guys, and the power-hungry officers who wanted to boss others around. Mobile Police Department officers, like all people, are multi-faceted. They aren't caricatures to fit neatly in boxes labeled "good cop" or "bad cop." I believe that a police department (like the rest of the world) is a mix of people, but it's the ones making poor choices that give the whole department a negative name. During my months around MPD, I have seen significantly more positive examples of officers than negative ones.

A couple of officers have told me they usually have ride-alongs who hate the police. The thought of them having to do a highly stressful job with someone breathing distrust beside them is nauseating. But the officers do it because it's part of the mantle they carry for the Mobile Police Department. MPD is welcoming to all those who wish to see how they work. At the time of this printing, you need to be over twenty-one years of age, live a drug-free/crime-free lifestyle, pass a background check, and be able to follow verbal directions.

On my first ride, as soon as the officer checked in with the dispatcher there was a call waiting for him involving a family. After assessing the scene, the officers said the child needed to be brought to the hospital, and a detective was called to meet the family there. Rather than go with the officer to the hospital, they decided I would switch to riding with the backing officer, and they had plans for me to move to a third officer later in the night.

I went with the flow and hoped I wasn't so annoying that the officers were pawning me off as soon as possible. There is the fact that my water bottle is notoriously squeaky every time I open and close it, but I have yet to hear of another civilian ride-along being treated as a "hot potato." I preferred to think of it as a symptom of the wonky squad dynamics (that I did learn afterwards was a documented issue for that specific squad), because on the final hand-off I was placed with the smiling officer from roll call, like they were sticking it to him by giving him the ride-along for half the night. (Both the officers I had ridden with were at the trade off, and yes, there was chuckling involved.)

The first thing the third officer did I when sat in his Tahoe was apologize for the aroma of the food he had just eaten for his midnight dinner, saying most people complained about the odors of his ethnic food.

"I don't mind," I assured him as garlic and other poignant smells lingered in the cab.

"I guess by now you figured out that nobody likes each other. I don't understand why. I don't have a problem with anyone."

And he wouldn't. Not with his glowing attitude and strong work ethic, which I hope he hasn't lost. After surviving the angsty roll call, it was a blessing to end the shift with positivity.

Out of all the hours I've ridden, I still consider those five and a half hours in his Tahoe as one of my favorite patrols.

Looking back, I refer to my first roll call group as a "reluctant squad," but that has been my only unsettling roll call experience.

When I reported to my second roll call in a different precinct the following month, I approached an officer about entering the building as a scheduled ride-along the same as before. The officer was friendly and obliging. As before, I was one of the first people in the room. This time, every officer who entered made eye contact and either spoke to or at least nodded and smiled at me. The officers were talking and joking amongst themselves until the leadership entered and announcements began. When the assignment to have me as a ride-along was given, the officer introduced himself with a friendly greeting.

At the third precinct I reported to during my academy months, the officer I approached in the parking lot to see about going into the building replied with a smile and said, "You're riding with me today."

I walked to the precinct door with him. When he saw me fidgeting on the way through the building, he said, "Relax. There's nothing to be worried about."

"I know," I replied. "I get nervous in new places."

On a return trip to one of the precincts, an officer ending his shift asked me, "Didn't you ride here before?"

I said I had several months previous.

"I remember you! You brought us snacks."

I've been in roll call rooms with as many as eighteen MPD personnel and as few as two. I've seen squads without a lieutenant or functioning without a sergeant, though the largest squads tend to have a lieutenant, one or two sergeants, and possibly a corporal or two. Each gathering is unique with the different tones the squads bring to the start of their day. Only once did I walk into a roll call room when the squad leadership was already seated. Things were so chill, the lieutenant was nearly sprawled in the chair; no posturing to convey authority. It was like a club they were all a part of, though if the lieutenant or sergeant gave directions, the officers followed them without question.

Most roll call rooms have been positive spaces, even when the lieutenant or sergeant is giving bleak reminders. They always go over a safety point, like how to approach a building when serving papers or for the officer to put on their reflective vest when working traffic accidents. And they will also share news about possible happenings due to civil unrest or holidays.

For example, toward the end of the roll call meeting one morning, the squad lieutenant mentioned it was Nine-Eleven. Then he went on to say that most of the officers in the room weren't born yet or if they were, probably didn't have a firm recollection of that day's world-changing events, but to expect to see some people waving, smiling, or even thanking them as a show of appreciation to first responders. When he mentioned the public might even be nice to them, one officer scoffed and muttered, "That'd be a miracle."

Hearing that remark reminded me that it can be a thankless and harrowing job the men and women in uniform signed up for even though it's one of the most mentally, emotionally, and physically challenging careers available.

Before dismissing roll call, the squad lieutenant or sergeant running the meeting will sometimes open the floor to anyone who wants to bring up what's on their mind. There has been shuffling of feet or paper, a sigh or muttered words. But even if nothing is spoken, there is an inkling of vulnerability in the room amid the pause. If an officer brings something up, a nervous laugh or grumble by another officer is a normal response. Sometimes it's an unofficial seconding of the opinion or question. Once that topic is addressed, a "Stay safe out there" or similar dismissal is given and each officer or training team goes out to their vehicle to sign in with dispatch. And sometimes there's a civilian ride-along following them to the parking lot.

2. Community is Key

"One of the marvelous things about community is that it enables us to welcome and help people in a way we couldn't as individuals."
– Jean Vanier

I have never been the type of person who craved social experiences. Writing is often synonymous with introverts, and that is for sure the situation in my case. Mingling with people in my family, church group, literary circle, or on the job was the average extent of my outreach. And don't even mention "small talk." It's not something I've ever been able to do without great pains—for myself and probably the person I'm trying to be polite with. After living in the same subdivision for decades, I only know a handful of neighbors by name.

When I joined the Citizens Police Academy, my whole outlook began to shift. The academy class was a wide sampling of people from across the county who worked or had retired from various professions. The age range spanned six decades and the members were all there for different reasons. Rather than sit in the back and stay quiet—my default maneuver in classes—I took a front row seat and tried talking to people and asking questions rather than just listening. I carried that level of engagement over to my ride-alongs and have since attempted to do so in general life.

One day, a sergeant's roll call reminder before the officers left on patrol was about the information they are supposed to collect at each incident. Having a thorough police report is important for many reasons, but the one highlighted that day was if the situation was passed to a detective, they would need a solid starting point. The patrol officers must collect the who, what, where, when, why, and how the event occurred. They are the front line of information collection, but detectives will follow through and dig deeper when merited.

As a writer, the why questions are an important factor to me. I want to understand what drives people to do things, which is one of the reasons I started doing ride-alongs. Even if they have their suspicions as to whom is at fault, the patrol officers write a neutral report because it's not their job to speculate. That being said, I've gotten into plenty of "what if" discussions with my hosting officers after a call because it's human nature to want to understand why things happen. Several of the officers I've ridden with have mentioned they want to go into investigative work so they can see the other side of the cases they only touch the surface of during patrol.

If there isn't a call waiting for the officer when they reach their patrol vehicle, they typically head to one of two places at the start of shift: their regular beat area to patrol or towards the nearest city fuel station to top off their tank. Not all the precincts have fuel pumps in their area, so there is a need for the officers to travel outside their regular boundaries to fuel up. When that happens, they inform Communication (the dispatchers) where they are going when they reach the precinct line, then again once they are back in their regular area.

So far, my tally of patrol vehicles is all Chevy Tahoes (SUVs) except for one Chevy Caprice (sedan). When it comes to patrolling, I feel more comfortable in a Tahoe because we are more visible when riding code (lights and sirens), and it gives a better vantage point. Other drivers being able to see you approach when driving code helps them clear the road. As for the line of sight, the view is helpful in areas with parked vehicles, crowds, or barriers like bushes when patrolling for potential issues. The sedan didn't handle speed bumps or potholes well, which slowed the officer considerably on the way to calls. A few officers have told me the slowdowns in the sedan inhibit chases, but at the time of getting this ready for publication, I haven't experienced a pursuit in either circumstance.

An MPD patrol officer's "office" is their vehicle. It has a computer, a (sometimes) working printer, copies of report forms, fingerprinting kits, riot gear, and more. Their "desk" is typically the passenger seat. Lots of officers use an organizer that hangs from the back of it so they can easily grab the proper item. That organizer is moved to the back of the vehicle when there is a ride-along, but their muscle-memory has the officer turning toward me before they laugh or sigh and get out of the vehicle to collect the proper paper.

With the need to do so much paperwork (even if it's on a computer), most officers will stop in a parking lot near a road when they compile things. It can sometimes look like they are doing nothing or goofing off on their computer, but they are writing reports or charting a traffic accident diagrams. Sometimes they will take a couple of minutes to eat or possibly call home before dispatch hits them with another call because they don't get an official lunch break. They snag time when they can because they are always on duty during their twelve-hour shift. That radio is constantly on to hear from Communication, even when using the bathroom. And yes, I've seen officers hurrying out of convenience stores saying, "We've got a call" when a minute ago they wanted to buy a drink. At least they were able to relieve themselves before we dashed out.

People tend to watch police vehicles drive by. Sometimes there's an automatic smile, wave, or nod of thanks when the officers pass. Other times it's a glare of uncertainty or suspicion. One time when on a call to assist a stranded motorist blocking a travel lane, the lady asked the officer who I was. (I suppose a non-uniformed, middle-aged lady sitting in the passenger seat of a police vehicle is unusual.) When the officer replied I was from the Citizens Police Academy, she came over to ask me about the experience.

"It's better than Girl Scouts," is what I always say. (I spent several years during my youth in the Girl Scout program. With the academy's class time, hands-on activities—like dusting for fingerprints and range day, and field trips like those to the 9-1-1 Call Center and horse barn, it had a similar feel to me.)

Stranded motorists and accidents are everywhere across the city, from the interstates to major intersections to back roads. They occur rain or shine, day and night. Minor accidents only require one responding officer, unless they are at night or on the interstate. For complicated accidents, including those blocking the street, more people are involved. I've witnessed MPD officers working alongside Mobile Fire Rescue Department (MFRD), Alabama Department of Transportation (ALDOT) employees, and tow truck drivers dozens of times. Each has a different role to assist the crash victims. MFRD crews pry open vehicles if doors are crunched shut and sprinkle granules of oil dry to absorb any fluid leaks from the engine components while their medical workers assess the victims.

ALDOT's Alabama Service and Assistance Patrol (ASAP) provides a large visual reminder in their lighted ASAP marked trucks, with flashing arrows signaling approaching motorists to move over on the interstates or highways in hopes of keeping both the first responders and the victims safer. The tow truck drivers move the inoperable vehicles and clear debris from the roadways with brooms or snow shovels. Though the dance is consistent, the community of first responders' tempo changes at each scene.

Patrolling the officer's beat area and talking with the residents or business owners within those boundaries is the pinnacle of policing the public wants to see in a perfect world. Communities feel safer when they notice officers regularly driving their neighborhood because criminal activity drops when there is a law enforcement presence. If police staffing is short (like it was during the years I rode) and call volumes high (also the case), that level of security can diminish and people might lose trust in the work MPD is doing because they aren't seeing officers "on the beat."

Besides valid calls, the officers are tied up handling false alarms on buildings, 9-1-1 hang ups, nuisance calls about animals or noisy neighbors, and civil complaints the officers aren't allowed to get involved in (though they will respond to the request to come) rather than patrolling. With the exception of Central Precinct because of its compact size in the downtown business/entertainment district, all of my shifts with MPD officers in 2024 and 2025 had us on calls outside of their patrol beats over half of the time because the officers were covering an area without a patrol unit either due to staffing shortages/days off, the officer for that area was working a different call, or they were the backing unit for another officer.

It's those familiar faces in patrol vehicles around town that strengthen connections between the community and the officers. At least one officer I rode with kept a basketball in the back of his Tahoe. He had a large city park and a couple of schools in his beat. If he didn't have a call and came across kids or teens in those spaces, he joined them for a game of basketball. Unfortunately, the day I rode left no room for play amid the traffic and domestic issues we were dispatched to.

Riding not only the well-known roads but also venturing into neighborhoods I had never visited during nearly three decades of living in the city of Mobile showed me the parallel worlds Mobilians live in. It's no wonder there are divisions politically and socially when less than ten miles can separate a flourishing park filled with people of all ages playing and exercising versus a beautifully updated park that residents are scared to utilize because of the potential for gunfire in the neighborhood. While police officers cannot control any individual's choices, there is the belief that increased police presence would allow more people to enjoy the green spaces the City of Mobile provides without fear.

Neighborhood concerns go beyond the obvious situation of blight, which is seen from the business district downtown to neighborhoods in West Mobile. When houses or store fronts are not usable because they are located in crime and litter-laden areas, will owners pay money for upkeep to an empty unit? Besides losing historic buildings to rot, apathy can set in. Neighbors might give up trying, one by one. The potential is there, but Mobilians need support from the community at large. The police department is often tasked with weaving that gap closed. It's a heavy responsibility that those working aren't paid nearly enough to carry, or even trained to handle in some cases. But most of them try the best they can each time they put on their badge.

Even when people feel safe, crime can happen. Every week in recent years, unlocked vehicles around Mobile had money, firearms, medications, and more stolen out of them. One morning, I watched an officer collect fingerprints off an unlocked vehicle where a thousand dollars was supposedly stolen during the night while it was parked in an un-gated driveway in an affluent neighborhood. Crime can happen anywhere. Please take a half a second to tap the lock button on a key fob or whatever means your vehicle takes to secure it. It's a lot less time consuming than a police report and dealing with stolen property.

Officers can have multiple run-ins with the same suspects or victims who have mental health issues, unhealthy home environments, or other problems relating to quality of life within their patrol area. They get to know the troubled individuals in their beat, whether they want to or not. I've seen multiple officers give water to homeless people when they stop to talk to them about a disorderly call. The men and women in blue have extended offers of rides to the crisis center or other assistance to those who show a decline in their cognitive abilities or increase in their stress levels. And with repeated domestic violence issues between adults, the officers who take the call extend assistance to the victim, in hopes that they will accept the help.

When between calls or on the way to a non-emergency issue and there is no activity on the radio, I like to chat with the officers while they drive. I have a handful of standard questions I ask such as, "Did you grow up here," "How long have you been an officer," and "Is there a special unit you want to work in?" From those answers or the different situations at the calls, more questions arise. I never disclosed specific information in my articles, but it was key for me to understanding the various mindsets and personalities that make up the Mobile Police Department.

I will note that I have ridden with MPD officers ranging in age from twenty-one to their mid-fifties, from diverse ethnic backgrounds, and with anywhere from less than a year to thirty years of patrol time. The men and women have been single, married, divorced, parents, continuing their education with college courses, working side jobs, business owners, former or current military members, and so much more. Some live in their precinct area, others across town or out of the jurisdiction. Many graduated from local high schools, others grew up in different parts of Alabama, several are from out of state, and a couple were born on different continents. The officers that listen to music while patrolling have had soul, country, rap, metal, and everything in between playing on the stereo. There's too much variety to list all their likes or life situations, but chances are the officers will share several things in common with anyone they have contact with, which can help build a bridge of understanding and compassion. Though they are all wearing a matching MPD uniform, they are a variety of people who all happened to dedicate their career to serving the community.

Observing the officers interact with the public is even more enlightening than Q and A time. One skillset many officers have is adapting their manners to meet the needs, ages, and situations of those they are assisting or confronting. It can be as drastic as submissive body posture—chin down, head tilted as though listening to his Nana give instructions for chores—while one officer was assisting a senior couple. Then he changed to chin up, shoulders squared, hands on belt as he approached an attractive woman with car trouble minutes later. He peacocked his uniform and knew how to work that swagger. I couldn't help smirking as I shook my head.

There are officers who have no hesitation in squatting down to talk to a young child. Others will adjust the way they speak to address a crowd of teenagers leaving a party to tell them to clear the road and get home safely in a way that doesn't come across as dictatorial. During disputes between neighbors or while collecting accident information, officers stay neutral and give both parties equal attention and respect even if they don't trust them. I have heard from officers that they think one or both parties were lying when giving their statements, but that does not change how they deal with them.

Not all officers have the same level of social graces as the next. Some are awkward because they are new to the job, and others might not be blessed with smooth people skills (which I completely relate to). Plus, officers get frustrated. Can it come across as rude or short tempered at times? Yes. I've witnessed an officer sounding slightly dismissive when questioning a woman to clarify her statements while we waited for an ambulance to arrive. It was the only assistance she was willing to accept because her preferred methods were not available to her (they were against Department policy). She became offended and stomped away while cussing out the officer, the police in general, and me for standing there and doing nothing.

During another incident, the responding officers were trying to get statements from the parties involved, but the individual they were questioning refused to answer the direct yes/no questions. Instead, the person yelled, paced, and waved their arms around while rehashing a previous version of the event. After the third attempt to question, the person moved toward their vehicle. When the officer stepped a few paces toward the vehicle, too, and repeated his question in a calm manner, he was accused of being aggressive and intimidating. A supervisor was requested so a complaint could be made. The lieutenant came and heard the grievances, taking everything in and making sure the person left feeling better after having vented, like management at a retail job might do for a customer.

As for the MPD officers themselves, most officers have preferred call types or those that they handle only because it's part of the job even though it's not an aspect they enjoy. Some officers love working traffic accidents, from getting each detail on the diagrams perfect to compiling the reports. Others want to help families or domestic violence victims break out of toxic environments, while others want to get dealers off the streets.

Officers will show their frustrations over annoyances or frustrations once they are back in their vehicle or in the precinct. Things like pounding the steering wheel, commiserating about a couple whose house they are repeatedly called to for domestic violence issues but the victim refuses to press charges, or complaining about "rent-a-cops," the private security people who deck themselves out like officers but have no authority. Many officers, especially on my return trips to squads, don't hold their opinions back though I'm sitting beside them.

Leadership has told me that it's both good and bad that the officers are so comfortable around me. I'm glad they are.

Several times a year, there are free events with first responders where the community can interact with police officers, fire fighters, and other emergency workers. Mobilians can speak to the officers, pet the horses from the Mounted Unit, sit on one of the Harley-Davidson motorcycles the Traffic Unit drives, and even watch the SWAT robot display its dexterity. MPD's daily patrols and maneuvers are far outside of these community events which show them engaging with the public on a professional, though staged level. Despite the stresses of work days, they do their best to be good ambassadors to the badge, though they sometimes fall short. They are reminded of the mantle they carry at the start of every shift by squad leadership. Some precincts even have

"Ride for the Brand" signs up. But the officers are human. They have good hours and rough days like the rest of us. Unfortunately their bad days have higher stakes than most other professions.

The majority of the time (nine out of twelve officers, so far), I'm old enough to be the mother of the officer I'm riding with. And wouldn't you know it, one of the times I wasn't, the officer was asked by a teen, "Is that your mama riding with you?"

When I asked one officer if he grew up here, he told me the name of the local high school he attended and said, "I graduated in nineteen."

There was a long pause because I was waiting for him to follow it up with ninety-nine or something. It felt like a minute later, but it was probably only seconds before it dawned on me he meant 2019.

I quickly said, "Oh, my nephew graduated from there last year," while thinking that I was old enough to be his mother. And he seemed so mature. Proof I'm older than I think I am!

When officers are close in age to my own children, it's difficult not to feel like a mother bear riding with them. Though they're the ones with months of training and a handgun on their hip, I have a natural defensiveness about the officers when they're being disrespected or in potential danger. If I didn't keep it internalized, I would have broken the ride-long rules while I was still in the Citizens Police Academy.

I felt the urge to protect the strongest during a scene of attempted intimidation. It was also the only time that I've felt scared during a ride-along. The incident took place after one in the morning on a sultry weekend night. A man and woman were walking down the yellow lines of a service road. The young officer I was with pulled up beside them, rolled down his window, and let them know they needed to get out of the middle of the road for safety reasons.

The couple came closer, the dreadlocked man who looked at least a decade older than the officer stared while the woman chatted. She apologized repeatedly, asked the officer's name, and said to have a good night before swaying her way to the shoulder of the road. The man continued to stare inside the Tahoe from his position on the center lines. The officer repeated that that man needed to get out of the street.

The man stepped closer, which caused him to lean down a bit to maintain eye contact through the window. His ornate bone necklace swung away from his shirt with the movement. It was easy to gauge he had almost a foot of height on the officer I was riding with based on how his body lined up next to the Tahoe.

Again, the officer advised the man to get out of the roadway.

Noncompliant, the subject stared back, looming closer. His eyes looked from the officer to me and back several times before he asked for the officer's name. Then his badge number.

The officer answered, then told him in a sterner voice to get out of the road.

The man's harsh gaze continued. I half-expected his hand to reach in and grab the officer by the throat. Yes, possibly a writer's overactive imagination at work, but the vile feelings flowing from him were tangible.

In my head, I prayed words of protection in between the mantra of "Don't hurt my boy. Don't hurt my boy. Don't hurt my boy."

The officer repeated the order to leave the road and slightly shifted in his seat as he unbuckled his seatbelt.

The man's dark look intensified, but I focused on faith to combat the vibes that I could only explain felt like hexes. Slowly, the subject stepped back, still staring at the officer. He sauntered in front of the Tahoe as though daring my host to hit the gas. I doubt he could see us clearly with the headlights on him, but that oppressive gaze was turned on us until he reconvened with the lady on the side of the road. The officer watched them a moment before driving away.

I can't remember exactly what we said to each other, but it was basically "that was intense." The officer mentioned that if I hadn't been with him, he would have gotten out of the vehicle and made the man comply sooner, but he didn't want to do anything that might have caused potential danger to me. As unsettling as the situation was, the officer's choice to stay in the vehicle that night reminded me how dangerous their patrol job is even on a seemingly mundane stop.

Since going through the Mobile Citizens Police Academy, I see the city by precincts. When I drive over the invisible line, my mind automatically switches to the events I saw when I rode there. When I see a Tahoe, I try to read the patrol numbers to check if it's someone I know. Usually it's not, but I have recognized a few officers by patrol number or sight. Some days I stay in my home precinct, but I typically journey within several, if not all five of them, while on errands. Since I know what to expect if I ever need to interact with the officers during a traffic situation or an emergency, I no longer dread having to talk with what I used to think were likely to be corrupt cops. Knowledge and experience are key to building understanding and community.

The four main precincts all meet on the Airport Boulevard overpass of Interstate-65. It's Mobile's own version of "Four Corners." First Precinct has the southeast section, on the eastbound side of Airport Boulevard where the Bel Air Mall property is, and on to the south and east. Second Precinct is the other southern half of the overpass bridge, towards the hotels and restaurants across I-65 from Bel Air Mall to the west. Third Precinct is the northeast, Springdale Mall side, and Fourth Precinct is across from that, with the westbound Airport Boulevard traffic and northwest area of the city toward Spring Hill and beyond.

One morning around 3:30 a.m., the officer I was with pulled over a driver who was playing loud music and didn't have a working license plate light on Airport Boulevard right before the I-65 overpass. About the time the backing unit arrived, the rookie officer found out the driver's license and car tag were expired too. Shortly after verifying the driver was not someone with priors, the backing unit's regular back-up arrived, followed by an officer from the neighboring precinct who shared that side of I-65. As more officers arrived, I thought for sure we would be taking the driver to the sally port.

That didn't happen.

Now, instead of assuming that a driver pulled to the side of the road at night must be "really bad" to merit two patrol units, I know that's the department's norm. And if there are three or more units, my first thought is it must be a tad slow on calls because the officers are seeking the chance to socialize. They look out for each other, even across precinct boundaries.

During a slow hour after midnight, about half of a squad ended up in a Waffle House parking lot while an officer was testing a driver's sobriety after the individual had crashed into a parked car. To the people driving by, it probably looked like a drug bust or post-violent criminal antics with half a dozen MPD vehicles on the property, but the driver was compliant, though tipsy. It was the officers seeking a few minutes of connection amid a long night on patrol. After a bit of chitchat and making sure the rookie responding officer and the backing unit had things under control, the extra officers headed back to their beats, one by one.

One shift, my host got a phone call from a squad mate who was having vehicle issues. After she told him which parking lot she was in, we headed over. Unable to locate the Tahoe's problem, we followed her to the precinct in case she had trouble along the way because he didn't want his squad sister (who was barely of legal age to walk into a bar) alone if the vehicle broke down in the predawn hour. Chivalry isn't dead.

Calls dispatched at night (and many issued during the day) require a backing unit. Officers working beats close to each other are paired up in most cases, but if a nearby one is already on a call, there might be a longer wait for the second unit to arrive. It can take a while to warm up to new faces, even amid the police family, but once established, those working bonds are strong. Officers will mention missing a squad member that transferred precincts or departments for months afterwards.

But the precinct boundaries aren't "do not cross zones." Units are sent to calls in other areas because a squad is over-extended or there is a need for specific help that an officer on duty in a different precinct can assist with, like foreign language translation. The "Port City" is an international destination for people traveling for business and pleasure, and the residents a typical melting pot of American life fusing many cultures into the fabric of what makes Mobile so special.

On one overnight shift, a handful of officers from the squad I was with happened across a pair of officers from the neighboring precinct at three-thirty in the morning. They all sat together in the restaurant near the precinct border, chatting and decompressing for a bit while eating "dinner."

A couple of times, I've witnessed the officers race across precinct boundaries to assist other squads when a distress call is placed over the radio. Once, the cross-precinct dash happened on a night shift. An officer radioed that he'd been exposed to Fentanyl while searching a suspect. He administered Narcan to himself but still felt sick. Being close to the precinct boundary where the distress call came from, the officer I was with ran code for ten blocks, pulling up seconds before MFRD and minutes before the backing units from the officer's own precinct.

The other time was on a day shift. Dispatch came over the radio with "shots fired" at a medical facility on a road that was in the adjacent precinct. Before moving forward, I want to explain that I have heard banter and gripes from both Communications (the phone/radio operators who dispatch the officers to calls) and patrol officers because they each think the other does not understand how stressful their jobs are. One group is tasked with trying to collect information from emotionally distraught people to pass along to the officers so they know what they are walking into. The dispatchers sometimes need to talk to the caller until help arrives or listen to the person on the phone take their final breath.

The officers physically handle the scene, with all the emotions and possible carnage. They both have it rough!

When the shots fired report came over the radio, the officer I was with exhaled a deep breath and hit his lights and sirens.

Before we got to the nearest intersection, two more MPD units barreled onto the road from a side street. As we passed the next major intersection, I spotted another Tahoe running code half a mile ahead of us. At least six units rode caravan with lights and sirens, listening to the Communications operator give updates—the only radio chatter allowed during times of crisis until an officer is on the scene.

We quickly learned the incident wasn't at the medical location previously mentioned, but next door at another clinic. Other fragmented details emerged every ten or fifteen seconds as the operator relayed what they were getting from the caller on the phone.

Visions of every single cop show and movie I've seen started flashing through my mind. I imagined the maneuvers involved in taking out an active gunman while familiar buildings blurred past at speeds never before experienced on those roads. I forced the images out of my head and visually followed the gentle rise of the road as we sped up one of the few hilly sections in the precinct. Concentrating on my breathing, I sat silently, trying not to let the officer's adrenaline spike affect me. I made sure my fingers were relaxed, hands loose, and stretched my jaw because the body holds tension in those areas.

About a mile after we crossed into the other precinct, the voice on the radio canceled the shots fired call, stating no additional units were needed.

Our speed dropped.

The dispatcher said a crying patient in the backroom of the second facility was the one who had made the call.

The Tahoe's lights and siren went off.

Another big exhale from the officer beside me. Then it was back to patrol with a shadow of what might have happened.

In addition to their regular patrols, officers from all over the city work overtime hours in the Entertainment District at night and during special events, like Mardi Gras. While the regular squad members downtown continue their duties that include things like barricade placement/removal, perimeter patrol, and traffic accidents, the overtime officers help keep eyes on the crowds flowing between bars and entertainment venues. MPD officers from different precincts fall into formation as though they have worked together daily when an altercation breaks out. Continued training and hands-on experience coupled with strong squad leadership and a desire to protect the community keeps them efficient.

It's up to leadership to follow through with training and to correct errors, whether big or small. As previously mentioned, training briefs are done during roll calls on a squad level, but it goes beyond those few minutes. For example, some leaders will kick back a report to an officer for them to fix, using it as a teaching point to assist the officer with their report if there is an issue they might be new to or working a rare call situation. At the end of the day, every-thing has the potential to reflect positively or negatively on the Mobile Police Department as a whole rather than a single officer who made an error.

They are in it together.

3. Kindness Goes a Long Way

"No kind action ever stops with itself. One kind action leads to another."
— Amelia Earhart

Every month, there are a smattering of news reports or social media posts about police officers who help someone mow their lawn, change a flat tire, rescue a kitten out of a tree, or other such obvious acts of kindness. But every day there are plenty of unsung acts done by Mobile Police Department officers. One time after twilight, I was the only one there to see an officer move an oak tree branch off a quiet neighborhood street. Making sure roadways are safe is part of their job, but it was extra important because the branch was lying in the travel lane just beyond a curve in an unlit section of the block. On another patrol just after dawn, an officer stopped to help a turtle cross the road. Minor incidents? Not to the next person who rounded the corner because a hazard was averted. Nor to the turtle who continued safely to its destination or the motorist who potentially swerved to avoid it.

MPD officers assist at traffic accidents around town and up to three miles beyond the city limit. Heat, rain, snow, and more do not deter the officers from being on scene. They might not want to be standing roadside any more than you would be, but they are there to see the situation resolved until the final tow truck pulls away. And if it's car trouble that has stalled a vehicle, there will often be attempts to assist before the tow trucks arrive (even if they aren't successful). I've seen officers push a vehicle off the road and jumpstart batteries, all while saying, "We aren't supposed to do this, but I can't just leave you here." If it's something they would personally do to help a stranger when off duty, they don't want to skimp on it while in uniform.

One summer afternoon, an officer drove under an I-65 overpass looking for a stalled vehicle he had been dispatched to even though it was just outside of his precinct. When turning around to go back for another look because we didn't see the car, he spotted an elderly couple who looked upset in the parking lot of a corner gas station. Thinking they could be the people with a faulty vehicle, he parked so he could talk with them. He found out they were confused about the receipt for their gas, afraid they were being double charged on their credit card. The officer went inside to speak to the attendant and then explained the situation to the senior couple. They left with smiles and a plethora of thanks all because an officer took a few minutes to investigate their frustration.

Throughout the year, MPD does teddy bear drives to collect cuddly animals for the officers to gift to children during stressful situations. The first time I witnessed a teddy bear handout was during a call regarding a gun being waved at a residence by a known suspect. The officer I was with was the backing unit, and he hung out at the foot of the steps. A young mother was on the front stoop, holding a baby on her hip, as the responding officer stood on the lawn, listening to her story and taking notes under the lone porch light. Every minute or so, a toddler and preschooler would push out of the screen door, run circles around their mother, and tug at her clothes.

"Mama! Mama! Mama!" they chanted, their braided hair bouncing as much as their bodies.

After this happened a couple of times, the backing officer spoke to the mother, then the children. He picked up the younger of the two with practiced ease and held the eldest's hand to bring them to the back of his Tahoe where he presented the bag of teddy bears.

"Go ahead and pick one," I heard him say. "And get one for the baby."

Squeals of delight filled the street before they dashed back to their mother and settled down with their new fluffy friends. It wasn't an earth-changing event, but it generated an ounce of peace during a stressful situation. Seeing the joy it brought those children cemented my participation in future stuffed animal drives.

"You're a father, aren't you?" I asked when he climbed behind the wheel.

He nodded and smiled, telling me how many he had at home.

"I figured you were by the way you handled the kids," I replied. "That was great."

But officers make mistakes, choose unwisely, and know others do as well. None of the Mobile Police Department officers I've ridden with want to go after someone for speeding a few miles over the posted limit or ticket someone for things they've done themselves. That subjectiveness varies by officer as they each have different life experiences and tolerance levels, but they've all been diplomatic about their position in law enforcement.

Sure, you think, but MPD leadership decides who you ride with. They aren't going to put a writer with a power-hungry jerk. That's probably true, but I've seen officers who enjoy pulling over drivers for traffic violations issue warnings and brief educational information with regards to the law rather than ticket the drivers in about three-fourths of the circumstances, regardless of who the driver was. If a vehicle tag is only slightly expired, the driver gets a "Take care of it within the next week," so long as their license and everything else is good. Or a "Don't use your phone while driving so you can keep your hands on the wheel." And also "You have to clear the intersection before the light turns green for the other drivers or it counts as running the red light."

People have valid concerns when they see drivers with phones in their hands, vehicles speeding through red lights, and other such incidents. "Where's a cop when you need one?" or "If I were a cop, I'd—" or even "Why don't the police notice expired tags?" are spoken out of frustration. I know, because I said things like that before I started doing ride-alongs.

The police can't be everywhere at once. Most officers do notice license plate tags when patrolling, particularly when stopped at an intersection behind someone with an expired one, but without enough units to answer the volume of calls, they don't have proper patrol time. MPD officers are busy dealing with false alarms, 9-1-1 hang ups, and nuisance calls about wild animals, fighting dogs, noisy neighbors, or homeless people walking around in their underwear. If the call comes in, they go, even if it's just to say they can't help (like in the case of coyotes running through a neighborhood). And let's not forget that they're busy with traffic accidents, domestic violence issues, as well as shootings, assaults, and robberies. It's almost scary to see the amount of crimes and shots fired you never hear about unless you see them or the aftermath. The news doesn't report on half of what's going on in the city.

Most officers are doing the best they can with the hand they're dealt. Are there those who do the bare minimum or ignore issues because they don't want to bother with paperwork? Yes, especially if their printer isn't working because that means writing citations by hand. If you look for the bad things, there are plenty to point out. However, from what I saw, the positive were more numerous than the negative.

Once, on a daytime call to a dispute that had turned physical between neighbors, I watched my host officer work his way down a weathered apartment complex, collecting statements from those involved in the altercations and the witnesses. He was about a dozen years my junior and his backing officer looked like he had a few years on me. Their sergeant, hands on his hips and a couple decades with MPD under his belt, oversaw them from several feet away. (Squad sergeants will arrive on scene for potentially volatile calls to help prevent things from escalating or guide rookie officers through steps they might not have experience with, if needed.)

My host's dark hair must have been soaking up the heat from the glaring sun while I imagined the backing officer's balding head would soon be turning red. The windows behind them were dirty with several broken blinds. I remember noting the inhabitants were mostly in mismatched or ill-fitting clothes, including some in pajama bottoms though it was the middle of the afternoon.

"It looks like 'People of Walmart' out there," I unsympathetically remarked as the officer wiped the sweat off his forehead when he returned to the Tahoe with a few identification cards.

"They're doing the best they can," he replied as he typed driver's license numbers in on his computer. "Times are tough, but people do what they can with what they have."

"Yeah," I said sheepishly over being called out for my judgmental sarcasm. "You're right. It's tough."

My observations heightened when my host collected the written statements from the residents and listened to their final concerns under the blistering sun while I watched from the air-conditioned patrol vehicle. Even the sergeant had retreated to his Tahoe while the patrol officers finished their investigation. I felt (rightfully) chastised for my remark, but I took it as a learning moment. "With respect for everyone" is the Mobile Police Department's motto, but it's also a great reminder for all, including me.

In a world full of road rage, biased complaints, and assaults, foulness abounds. I've observed MPD officers deal with verbal abuse, attempted intimidation, and even physical attacks, but they keep doing their job as calmly as possible so they don't violate a person's rights or end up in a viral video. If the subject's noncompliance endangers themselves or someone else, or if it escalates to a physical attack, then the officers will subdue the threat.

One day, there was a man in a wheelchair who had allegedly made threats against customers in a store and damaged the building's automatic door while brandishing a screwdriver before leaving. When three officers confronted him, he accused them of lying and began a tirade of profanity-laced derogatory speech. The foul language poured in my open window as I watched the scene play out a dozen feet in front of me. The responding officers would ask a question, then the man would hurl hateful comments and racial slurs at them based on their profession or skin color before they calmly re-asked the unanswered question, unperturbed by the abuse.

My own agitation grew at the man's belligerence because the officers were going on the information they received from dispatch. The operators in Communications get their information from emotionally distraught people (who are known to misspeak in their agitation), but that's all the officers had to act on. The suspect berated them with every name imaginable, calling them liars because he didn't have the reported screwdriver. From my vantage point in the Tahoe, slightly back from the altercation, I could see a wrench clamped on the wheelchair, easily accessible to the subject. All the officers were too far away from me to inform them without drawing their attention away from the irate man.

I'm not a confrontational person, but I was ready to march over and tell him he didn't need to disrespect the officers when he knew he had a tool, even though it was different than the reported weapon. Being a stickler for rules, I kept my seatbelt on and my mouth closed because the two big rules as a ride-along are: you do not leave the vehicle without your officer clearing the location as safe, and you do not interact with subjects or witnesses.

A short while later, two out of the three officers on-scene handcuffed the subject. As soon as that was done, the man turned toward one of the officers.

The officer jumped back and yelled, "You tried to bite me!" while holding his forearm. "Why'd you try to bite me?" (There was an expletive in the last sentence, but under the circumstances, most people would consider that unavoidable.)

Seconds later, the other officer had the subject on the ground, scrambling to keep him under control as he thrashed around. The officer knelt on him to prevent him from physically assaulting anyone else. It did nothing to shut him up. Then he began spitting at them. The officer I was with retrieved a mesh spit hood out of his supplies, and there was a short struggle to put it on the subject. The specially designed hoods keep spit from being a projectile, though body fluid still oozes through the mesh.

As soon as the subject was in the back of a patrol vehicle (still spewing obscenities), the officers shook the tension off with a few jokes as they cleaned their arms and gear with disinfecting wipes. When EMS arrived on scene, they made sure the bite hadn't broken the skin of the officer . It didn't, which was good because when he was taken to the hospital for an exam before being brought to jail they found out the subject had contagious diseases.

When a squad leader arrived, I motioned him to my window and pointed to the wheelchair. "There's a wrench clamped to it just under the armrest. That's probably the weapon he used."

He nodded in agreement and joined the arresting officers.

"How can you keep going like nothing happened when people are talking to you guys like that?" I asked my host when he got back into the Tahoe. "He was making me mad, and I wasn't even on the receiving end."

"It happens every day. We make jokes about it and learn not to let it stick."

I cannot fathom having to endure barrages of animosity each day at work. I've seen men and women of a variety of ages shouting and cussing at officers, both on day and night shifts. Even after witnessing a charged encounter as a ride-along, the emotions linger. Yes, I'm empathetic to the point where I sometimes have to place mental walls up in order to not be overwhelmed by outside emotions, but a toxic environment is nothing to downplay, no matter if you're expected to let it slide.

Besides officers being on the receiving end of threatening behavior, seeing someone get searched is also uncomfortable for me to observe. Those seem like two very different things, but both instances involve the potential for things to rapidly go wrong due to the heightened emotions and/or the officers' close proximity to the subjects. I have seen people who were calm, crying, and also fighting while being searched. All of them made me squirm in my seat within the patrol vehicle or look away the one time I was standing outside the vehicle. Personal space is something I highly value, and in those moments, the subjects have none, no matter how respectfully the officers handle the situation.

Volatile relationships or family-related turmoil were easily in the top third by call volume when I was with MPD, in all precincts except Central. (With Central Precinct being only two miles wide in any direction and encompassing the business and entertainment districts, their residential numbers are the lowest in the city's precincts.) Often the officers are turned away at the door. Other times, the disagreement continues once the police arrive, spilling into the front yard under the blue glow of the patrol units' lights.

The loudest altercation I saw was when a mother-in-law got involved. I don't blame the dude for hiding in the back yard until the police arrived, because that woman wasn't holding anything back when it came to threatening the guy who had cheated on her grandbabies' mama.

While I have been cleared to enter one post-domestic call scene, I opted to stay in the vehicle because I didn't want to be overwhelmed by the emotions of a mother worrying over her hurt child. I know my limits, and while I appreciated the opportunity, I knew it wasn't one I was ready to experience.

One squad, upon knowing I had completed over fifty hours of ride-along time without even seeing an arrest, called for the officer I was with to join the other units on scene at a shoplifting situation. The adult was already arrested and in a vehicle, but while they waited for another guardian to arrive, they placed the juvenile who had been with the subject in the backseat of my patrol vehicle. Listening to her crying was heart-wrenching, to say the least. I was glad to see the teenager released to the other parent. Hopefully that fraction of an hour in the back of a police cruiser was the only time she'll ever spend there.

Another officer obliged my request to drive to my grandparents' old house which was in the precinct. I have fond memories of my childhood visits there, including sitting on the swing in the screened-in front porch of the house during afternoon thunderstorms that were frightening but magical for a California girl.

When I mentioned the nearest cross streets, the officer looked at me as if I was remembering wrong. Though it was once a safe area, over the last few decades it had been mentioned several times in news reports for shootings and gang brawls. I hadn't been back in over a dozen years.

"Right there," I told the officer as we passed the shotgun-style house in the pre-dawn morning. "That's where my grandparents lived. And next door were two great-aunts. There was a gate between the back yards, and we'd cross between the houses all the time. I spent hours on those porches when I was a kid."

"And what do you think?" he asked, not stopping as his gaze roamed the street.

"It looks better than I expected. It's been fixed up a little since the last time I saw it, but the aunts' house doesn't look good."

He got to the end of the road and drove into the dirt between brush and trees on tire tracks that had become an unofficial roundabout.

"I'm glad it's not abandoned," I said. "I hope the owners care for it."

I gazed at the location of my childhood memories once more on our way out, pleased one little house survived another decade rather than succumbing to blight. And I'm grateful to the officer who extended kindness to indulge my whim.

Repeatedly seeing officers doing their best to remain helpful amid times of stress has reminded me to look beyond myself and notice what I can do to help—whether it's as simple as holding the door open for someone, assisting a neighbor, or donating items to a group or individual in need. Every small act of kindness adds up. The officers extend a helping hand each time they encounter a person in need. Seeing that has reminded me to check in with my friends more often because we never know what people are dealing with behind closed doors. Focusing on the positive, on acts of service and compassion, rather than the negative in any aspect of life is empowering. The good is right in front of you when you are looking for it.

4. Embrace Humor

"A little comic relief in a discussion does no harm, however serious the topic may be."
– C.S. Lewis

The "brotherhood" of those in blue is real. It's a family, dysfunctions and all. Officers may grumble about each other, both subtly and not so subtly, but it's most often a mention of another officer being "all right" or a friend rather than complaints. It can also be a lot like high school. Cliques, adolescent humor, and people trying to one-up each other. Locker room-style jokes and teasing come with the territory, but the officers have each other's back because they are the only ones who understand the stresses of the job. Each day on patrol they see humanity at its worst rather than at its best. No matter how strong you are emotionally, it has the potential to break you down. They will joke to lighten the mood, commiserate with each other, or give a nod to signify that yeah, they get it. Some days suck.

Though I can be as sarcastic as anyone else, I am known for taking things literally. You can consider that one of many neurodivergent thinking patterns that give me a hint (or heap) of uniqueness depending on your own outlook. I need a bit of time to understand someone's sense of humor when they are new to me because I assume they are straightforward about everything. Why? Because I do not joke around with people until I am familiar with them. My brain thinks that is everyone's default setting because it should be. (That's probably more sardonic than sarcastic.) As you might guess, my mindset has proven awkward at times when riding with the police.

Officers utilize humor, including the type that might be considered dark or inappropriate to others. Fortunately, when it was obvious I thought they were serious because I didn't laugh or reply in kind, the officers told me it was a joke and gave me the information in a straightforward manner. I have learned to go into a new-to-me squad's roll call without taking things too seriously. When I am unsure if it's humor or not, I will do my best to smile and reply in a noncommittal way.

For instance, one of the officers I rode with asked me if I had good aim after hearing I had completed my range day. Coupled with his nod of approval over the location of the bullet holes in my target photo, he motioned toward his shotgun mounted between our seats.

"If something happens to me, my shotgun's right there."

"Okay…."

"But let's hope you don't need it."

I had no idea how to respond to that statement from an officer I had known for only a handful of minutes. Unsure if he was serious or joking, I was too surprised to ask. I gave a half-nod while trying to smile.

That was the second time an officer had told me about the shotgun, but it was the first time someone showed me how to release it from its holder. After a third officer gave me the shotgun speech, I told a multi-decade MPD veteran about it and asked if it was for real or a joke. He tried (unsuccessfully) to suppress a grin and admitted he had told riders something similar.

"But is it a joke or for real?" I asked, still confused.

"It's both. You can use the shotgun to defend yourself if—and only if—all three of these things happen. Your officer goes down, there are no other officers there to assist you, and you are personally under attack. Otherwise, don't touch it. It's the host's way to bring humor to a worst-case-scenario that we all need to plan for. Okay?"

I nodded, eyes wide, while thinking "Here's to hoping I never need it!"

Remember the officer I rode code with to the perceived "shots fired" call, which ended up being cancelled in-route? After heading back toward his precinct, he pulled into a shopping center parking lot a mile down the road. Another officer who had also been in the caravan pulled up beside him until their windows lined up and both rolled theirs down.

"Someone was tripping on anesthesia!" the other officer said with a laugh.

They joked for a minute or two until their adrenaline levels rebalanced. Nothing was said about their own emotions. But they both knew the other officer understood. Then it was back to business.

A lot of officers like to point out all the locations where they have seen dead bodies, especially their first. One officer made it feel like a haunted tour rather than a patrol with his commentary.

"My first body was there…and another was over there the same week…and a dead body in there… and one.…" The silence outside the patrol vehicle took on a new eeriness in the darkness.

On a different shift, a call over the radio that another unit was dispatched to caused my host to make a strange offer.

"That sounds like it might be a dead body call. We could go to it. Have you ever seen a dead body?"

"Not on patrol, but I've seen dead bodies." I smiled mischievously and offered no further explanation as to the relatives I had witness pass away while on hospice.

He flashed me an unsettled look and changed the subject. And no, he did not take me to the potential dead body location. To this day, I am not sure if that was a missed opportunity or not, but no dead body stories were told at the end of the shift, so I think it was a false alarm.

And let's not forget the "person down" calls or those spotted on the ground while on patrol. The officers always hope the person is just drunk or having a medical emergency rather than dead. One man sleeping alongside a shopping center was so contorted, he looked like a mannequin that had been folded into a suitcase. I thought for sure he wasn't a real person, but the officer called it in as a potential person down when requesting backup before approaching. It is amazing how quickly people sit up when they see a police officer standing over them.

One piece of advice I have is to never sneak up on a cop. Their guard is rarely down, but one night at a traffic stop with multiple units, my officer was running IDs on his computer. His window was down and another officer passed in front of the vehicle to ask him a question. Attention back on the computer screen, he didn't notice a second figure appear at his window after approaching from the rear of the vehicle.

I nodded hello to the newcomer, not wanting to break the concentration of my host.

After several seconds, the officer standing at the window said, "Whatcha doing?"

The officer in the driver's seat noticeably flinched, right hand going towards his holster as he turned to the window. Upon seeing his smiling friend at the door, he laid in with, "Do you know how close you were to being shot? Don't ever do that to me again, man!"

Which was replied with, "You should pay more attention" and a lot of laughter.

"What are you even doing over here?" my host asked, waving his hand toward the opposite side of the bridge. "You should be over there."

"It was lit up like Christmas over here, and I wanted to see what was going on." A bit of MPD antics in the early morning hours. Then he went over to the other officers to spread the story about how he made their squad brother jump out of his skin.

Another time, at the scene of a single-vehicle accident on a main road, traffic was steady even though it was close to midnight. About half an hour before, I had texted my husband to update him on my location and the type of call we were on, which is something I did if there were a few minutes to think outside of what was happening around me. When he got off work, he texted back to see if I was still there. I was sitting in the patrol vehicle and the officer was about fifteen feet in front of me, hanging out with the firefighters on the side of the road while they awaited the tow truck.

The backing MPD unit had gone to a more pressing call so the right-hand lane we were parked in (blue lights on) was clear behind us for several dozen feet until the nearest intersection. I saw my husband, John, pass in the opposite direction and flip a U-turn at the light. The firefighters and the officer immediately focused on the civilian vehicle that had just pulled up behind the Tahoe. When John's door opened, one of the firefighters elbowed the officer. They all stared as a burly, bearded guy exited the vehicle.

My hosting officer immediately started walking toward the Tahoe, body language conveying he meant business, complete with hands near the tools-of-the-trade encircling his waist. My husband strode toward the passenger side, and the handful of firefighters watched as though they were expecting a fight.

I lowered my window all the way, glancing from my husband at my door to the officer as he reached the hood of the Tahoe (getting out of the glare of the headlights). Leaning out the window, I kissed John and saw the officer's posture relax as he rounded the vehicle to the driver's side.

"I just got off work and wanted to give my wife a goodnight kiss," John said as the officer opened his door.

"Yeah, no problem. I'm getting my soda," the officer replied. He grabbed his beverage and headed back to the firemen, who eagerly awaited the news.

"You almost got taken out by MPD!" I told John. "He was just talking to the guys over there, but when you pulled up he went into action mode. You should have approached slower. He thought you were a threat. You look menacing in the dark. Did you see his body language?"

"Yeah, but I wasn't up to no good," John replied nonchalantly. "I was stopping to see my wife."

"He was ready to drop you!" I scoffed even if it was a relief to know the officer would immediately step up when he spotted a potential threat. Also, after nearly thirty years of marriage, I would honestly say John deserves a tase for all he's put me through. He would probably say the same thing about me.

Another time, an officer touched the answer button on his phone screen when climbing into the Tahoe after defusing a trespassing situation.

The breathy voice of his girlfriend filled the cab. "Hey, baby, how would you like—"

"Girl, wait up." He scrambled to get the phone out of the holder so fast, he barely managed to switch the speaker off before saying "I've got a ride-along with me. Let me call you after the shift. Yeah, I'll see you in about two hours."

Once, when I settled in the Tahoe for my first ride in a precinct, the officer said, "I've only totaled one vehicle."

"And that's good?" I asked as I secured my seatbelt.

"Yeah!"

I replied with a smile, but in my head it was a "bless your heart" moment. At least it wasn't the same officer who blasted "Highway to Hell" while running code in the middle of the night—one of many unforgettable moments during my ride-alongs.

There was a time when the first words out of an officer's mouth when approaching the subject of a call were, "What did I tell you about keeping your pants on?"

Or the deadpan remark to a man who had run out of gas in the turn lane of a major intersection of "Why did you do that? There's a gas station right across the street."

A different shift had an officer slowly driving toward us while we were parked in a shopping center to finish a report. The other officer rolled down his window as he drew up alongside the driver's door, puckered his lips, and blew a kiss at my host before laughing as he drove past. Grinning while shaking his head, the officer explained they had gone through the Police Academy together and that was just how it was between them: constant jokes.

And once there was chatter between squad mates when three units were called to a motel that had half a dozen private security guards standing around, scared to intervene when a knife-wielding resident barricaded himself in his room.

"You'd think with all that gear on they'd be able to figure things out without calling the real police," an officer said dismissively.

"If they're going to all that trouble to look like a cop," another added, "they might as well go through the Police Academy and be the real thing."

During the early morning hours of a night shift, an officer was required to check an abandoned building in his beat because a few doors to it were closed when they should have been opened (the regulation the property owner had in place). My host called for a fellow squad member to be his backup and waited for her to arrive. If there were meth users, homeless people, or gang members inside the building, he would deal with them, but he said it was more likely the wind that closed the doors. That meant there were probably just spiders inside, he informed me, but he did not mess with spiders. The female officer who arrived as back up opened the doors and went inside each of the rooms without hesitation while the officer with arachnophobia covered her from outside the door.

A squad who had just welcomed a new member for field training found out that the rookie lived a few blocks away from another squad member. They used the slow hour at two in the morning to set up a carpool between the established officer and rookie until the new guy got his own patrol vehicle. A third officer teased them about needing to wait a few days before scheduling their rendezvous. The ribbing about taking things slower went on several minutes. Was it a sign of adolescent-style humor or being overly punchy more than seven hours into the night shift? Probably both.

When an officer bemoaned a day shift was eerily quiet I said, "Blame my mother. I think she's praying too hard over my safety when I'm riding. That's probably why I've never been to the sally port."

"Tell her to knock it off," the officer said. "It's messing with my flow."

Police officers do not sign up for the job expecting to have nothing but boring shifts, that's just the reality of the job, but prayers for their safety are always welcomed. (Just not too many, Mom.)

One friend suggested I start throwing things at the police if I wanted to go to jail, forgetting that I preferred to be in the front seat, not the back, when I hitched a ride to the sally port.

Since joining the Mobile Citizens Police Academy Alumni Association, I make sure to bring snacks or drinks or both to roll call when I ride so the squad members can grab something for their shift. Once on a return trip to a precinct, a squad sergeant whose group I had ridden with the last time I was there happened to be the one who let me in the building. Seeing the boxes of snacks in my arms, he first teased me about bringing him treats and then for abandoning his squad for their counterpart like his team wasn't good enough for me.

"I need to mix things up sometimes," I replied while I followed him to the roll call room.

"I brought y'all something," he announced as he motioned me ahead.

After roll call, I was thanked multiple times by members on the squad for bringing "the good stuff."

"My teens tell me I feed MPD better than them," I replied. "I kept this stash in my car so I didn't have to listen to them complain this time."

One morning, I brought two dozen fresh doughnuts from a local shop I had passed on my way to the precinct. As the officers came in, several looked at the closed boxes with interest. The doughnuts sat untouched while the squad leaders conducted business.

When the officers were dismissed, one bravely flipped open a lid.

"There's maple bacon!"

A few crowded around while another officer lifted the second lid of assorted doughnuts.

The first officer looked at me. "Where did you say you were from?" he asked.

I turned toward him and pointed to the logo on my polo shirt. "Mobile Citizens Police Academy Alumni Association."

"Oh, good!" He grabbed a doughnut. "Because I was thinking you were from Communications. If that was the case, you might be trying to kill us."

At a different roll call, I dropped a cooler bag full of assorted sparkling juice and a box of snack-sized goodies on one of the tables. I sat back and watched as the officers entered and went to happily grab a chilled can. When they saw the unfamiliar logo, and that they were smaller than soda cans, several became vocal.

"What is this?"

"Is it like an energy drink?"

"Yes," I replied. "Natural energy."

A few snickered and a couple of brave officers chose a can and took it to their seats. Others peered in before giving it a wide berth.

"*Sparkling* juice?" someone asked.

"It means you have to drink it with your pinkie out," an officer replied, which got everyone laughing.

After the roll call was complete, there were yet more complaints and jokes about the sparkling juice, but some people grabbed one to take on the road and even more took from the bagged snack offerings. Not long after I left with my assigned officer, the squad leader called her cell phone to apologize for the lack of gratitude shown. It was fine, I assured him over the speaker. I found the whole situation as amusing as the officers had.

Once, I disastrously made the choice to bring mixed nut snacks and fresh oranges—protein and vitamin C.

A couple of hours after roll call, a mocking voice over the squad radio channel said, "Make sure you eat healthy, boys."

Even with the singsong voice, I recognized who it was. But memo heard, officer. Now whenever I bring fruit, I make sure there's junk food to go along with it.

Several times I have ridden with officers who, despite it being frowned on, like to have their backing unit on speaker phone. The long conversations have always been during night shifts, so it's possibly a way to stay awake between calls. I enjoy it because it gives me greater insight into the squad dynamics and showcases the personalities of more officers than just the one I am riding with.

Sometimes the officers share about a previous call they were dispatched to. Other times it can be a quick message from someone who was just dispatched as backing to a call, but they are stuck in a food line to buy their dinner, so they ask the officer to take the call for them. And since there's a third person listening, there might be questions directed to me or jokes about the ride-along situation.

One night was seasoned with reminders from a previous host to my current one that "We need to get her to metro." A different time it was "Are you doing okay, Miss Carrie?" and "Miss Carrie, what do you want to do next?" over the speaker. I kept asking to go to the sally port because I hadn't been there yet, but he didn't oblige the request with an arrest.

During my first night on patrol, the fellow officer asked my host "How's the ride-along lady?"

"She's cool," the officer I was with replied. "She's going to write a book about me."

"Yeah, right," the voice on the line replied.

"It's true. I'm the main inspiration for her character," he replied with a smile and glance at me.

I returned his smile but shook my head. I had just finished final edits on *Loyalty: Washington Square Secrets 3*. One of the main characters in it is Officer Jim Abbott, a beat cop in 1920 Mobile. I was watching the mannerism of the officers to make sure my Jim was authentic because the next book had even more MPD scenes and characters. But Jim Abbott was first introduced on page in *Severed Legacies*, which was released in 2022. That novel is set before Jim joined the Mobile Police Department, though his self-confidence and desire to help was noticeable even then.

But to that officer who wanted to be in a book, be careful what you wish for. You just might get it.

During an early morning, when there was about an hour left on the shift, the officer I was with was parked in a lot fronting a main road alongside a second patrol car, the drivers' windows lined up and rolled down. While they were finishing up reports and checking their phones, I was going through the photos I had taken to see which ones would be good to use on my blog. I deleted several and edited out identifying details in the pictures I was saving. One event had two photo options, and both officers were pictured in them. I passed my phone to my host and said to hand it over to the next officer after looking so they could both weigh in on the options.

"This one," the second officer said, "because my ass looks better in it."

Admittedly, it takes a high amount of self-confidence to put on a police uniform. The men and women who wear the badge of law enforcement deserve a base level of respect for doing the job a small fraction of the population would even attempt in the recent social climates. They've earned that swagger, though my presence might have tampered it down once or twice. Like the time I entered a convenience store at 11:30pm with my host officer to get drinks.

The lady working checkout looked between us quizzically and asked, "Are you going to be out with him all night?"

"Yes," I replied with a smile, "I'm keeping him in line."

The worker laughed and my host looked startled with a touch of embarrassment before smiling. And yes, I was old enough to be that officer's mother.

5. Check Off

*"I like to listen.
I have learned a great deal from listening carefully.
Most people never listen."*
–Ernest Hemingway

Just as they begin their day with reminders, the squad leadership will drop final tips and training before dismissing the officers. Often it is based on issues that came up during the shift. Reminders to stay up to date on vaccines because they never know what they will come into contact with, or admonishments to go over the radio with their location and what they are doing rather than just telling their buddy on the phone. If something goes wrong, dispatch and the squad leadership would not know where the officer is if they leave their vehicle.

Upon returning to the precinct at the end of the shift, I have been greeted several times by leadership saying something along the lines of "You made it!" when we gather at the check-off desk. While this might seem merely humorous, apparently the majority of riders don't do the full shift. Besides being a writer with a squeaky water bottle, I'm also a novelty for riding the whole patrol.

I want to mention that I have raised three kids so I know a thing or two about long days and sleepless nights, but usually by this time on a shift I'm doing good to put a complete sentence together. My peopling is maxed out, my introvert batteries nonexistent. And that is without factoring in sleep deprivation if it's been an overnight shift, even if I fell asleep for a few minutes. I have been known to nod off for a few minutes around three or four in the morning. The officers have been too polite to mention if I snore, but I'm pretty sure I have woken myself a few times because of it and have caught a few well-deserved grins or suppressed laughs. Maybe there needs to be a book written by MPD officers about their patrols with civilian ride-longs. I would totally read that!

On return visits to a squad, the leadership or one of my previous hosts have asked how it was this time. I think leadership is looking to see that my repeated rides continue to be informative. And in the case of a previous host, they are checking to see who did a better job between them and the latest officer. Each wants to offer the best experience, the most thrills. More of their competitive nature on display.

One evening, my hosting officer was the first one back to the precinct. After the squad sergeant expressed his surprise over me making it the full day, my officer complained about all the traffic accidents we were sent on and added, "At least she got to ride code once."

The sergeant's eyes nearly bulged. "You rode code with her? You're not supposed to ride code with a civilian! What if something were to happen?"

The officer stammered that he didn't know, and the sergeant started fussing again.

Feeling the officer's anguish, when the sergeant paused for breath, I butted in.

"I usually ride code at least once during a ride. I signed my waiver, so I can't sue if something happens."

"Good, because we don't have any money," the sergeant quipped. We all laughed—more of that humor in action to dispel the frustration. Then he turned back to the officer. "But be careful out there, use your judgment, especially with a civilian with you."

"Yes, sir," was the reply.

What else was there to say?

Commiserations and high points are shared as the officers return to the precinct. You can hear the same story multiple times as new arrivals want the scoop on the biggest call of the shift or even from the week. Surprisingly, the stories stay consistent. No bloated fish stories here. Is it because the officers are used to keeping to the facts or that they know their fellow officers will call bull if they vary too far because they had already heard part of it over the radio? I'm not sure, but I would be interested in hearing those same stories told to people outside MPD to see how they hold up.

I have seen officers begin acting like fraternity brothers at the end of the shift and talk about where they can go to unwind, what they could do.

"In this uniform," one said, "we ain't doing nothing."

(To which I say thanks for remembering you are all in this together because what you do, in uniform or out of it, reflects on the whole department.)

Other times, there is chatter about an event that did not have a satisfying resolution on their watch. Like subjects who got away on foot even with the K-9 unit on the call or multiple officers patrolling for hours. Stories like those can be accompanied by tales of other run-ins with the subject. Warnings from firsthand experience to help keep their brothers and sisters safe should they spot the subjects in the future. Once it was, "If you ever see him, do not approach alone" because the subject's known strength and fearlessness. He appeared scrawny but had bested officers twice his size in the past.

At check off on my final ride in 2025, the lieutenant greeted me with, "So you made it the full night."

My hosting officer said, "And we got her to metro!"

My previous host, whom we did a lot of backing on calls with and knew I wanted to make it to the sally port so I could get the full experience, added "We got her there on her thirteenth ride."

And they did, with perfect timing.

Within minutes of reaching my 150th hour on patrol, the massive metal garage door of the jail's sally port rolled up to allow the Tahoe entrance right about midnight. Once the door was closed, the officer exited the vehicle and opened the back seat door. Out stepped a polite man with a previous felony arrest and a parole violation that had caused a warrant to be issued for him. Even with the handcuffs and forthcoming trip to jail, he was secure about his current path and the work he was doing to change his life around. If everything happens at the right time for a certain reason, his arrest and any subsequent court dates might be the way to alleviate the shadow of his past choices so he can rise above it.

One evening, as the officers were gathering around the check-off counter, a precinct detective ushered a handcuffed subject inside the station toward the interrogation rooms. The guy in the handcuffs didn't look happy, and the expression on the detective's face wasn't much better.

I wanted to walk behind them and watch through one of the observation windows I had seen on a previous tour of the precinct. Instead, my eyes followed them until they rounded the corner while I held my position.

"That's what you want, isn't it?" my officer asked. "See an arrest and take the bad guy to jail."

"I want to see everything and experience all the possibilities of a patrol shift," I told her.

And for the most part, I have. Plus more than I imagined.

Sometimes when I ride, it's the squad's final day before their "weekend" (multiple days off in a row, no matter when it falls during the week.) When dismissed at the end of check off, there's a reminder to have fun but stay safe. For those getting off from a twelve-hour night shift during their work week, it's "Get some rest and I'll see you this afternoon." Nights are long, and those days they are supposed to rest seem super short in comparison.

No matter my level of alertness, one thing is always clear at the end of a shift: Mobile is ripe for help and healing. A difference can be made, one call at a time, even if the change is happening to those within the patrol vehicle. On each of my shifts, I have been enlightened by the officers of the Mobile Police Department and their interactions with the members of the community. Sometimes it is so subtle I don't realize it until months later when I notice my previous thought patterns, like the instantaneous negative judgements of strangers are no longer coloring all my internal narrative. I've found myself reacting with compassion more than un-charitableness. Other times, I know in the moment I witness officers helping without hesitation that I want that to be my first response in situations as well.

Thank you, officers, for reminding me to laugh, to be compassionate, and to serve the community with honor because we are each representing a greater good than we can ever be alone.

    Until the next roll call.

Acknowledgments

Though I do my writing alone, the finished book takes a small but mighty support team. From the reassurance of family, friends, and readers I drew encouragement to keep going. Special shout-outs to both the members of the Mobile Writers Guild and Dalby's Darklings (my private Facebook group.) Thanks for your curiosity and cheer.

During the second half of 2025, I was fortunate enough to cross paths with Bay Area watercolor artist Jacqueline Parks. Her inspired hand and keen eye were just what the cover art needed for this story. It was amazing to see how you took my random ideas to create the painting dripping with Mobile charm and police flare. Thank you, Jacqueline!

Candice Marley Conner is one of the few people I am comfortable showing my early drafts to. Thanks for continuing to wade through the grammatical errors to share your opinions with me. Billie Rowland was the first to see my completed manuscript. I appreciate you talking the time to read amid your busy schedule to check for accuracy in MPD terminology and policies. Then professional editor Sean Connell got a hold of it. He is blessed (or cursed) with being able to understand my visions, sort through the (sometimes unwritten) messages to find the heart of what I'm attempting to say, and guide me to utilize my literary strengths to tell the best possible version of each story. The reader-friendly finished product is due in large part to him. Finally Ted Johnson read through the polished draft to check again for MPD accuracy. Thank you for your assistance.

A huge thank you goes to the Mobile Police Department for allowing me to ride shotgun with their remarkable officers. I hope I've done justice, both in the online articles and within these pages, in expressing the scope of the diverse tasks the officers are challenged with each time they report for duty. And to each of the officers I've ridden with, I appreciate all you've taught me through words and actions.

For More Information

If you are curious about the workings of the Mobile Police Department, I highly suggest going through MPD's Citizens Police Academy and then utilizing the Civilian Ride-Along program. You can apply to ride without going through the academy, but you'll get more out of the experience if you do both. Links to applications for the Citizen Police Academy and the Civilian Ride-Along option can be found on MPD's website under the PROGRAMS tab. https://www.mobilepd.org/ If you are not in the Mobile area, check with your local police department for similar programs in your jurisdiction.

To read more information about the history of MPD, I recommend *Unbroken Service:*

A History of the Mobile Police Department by Billie L. Rowland. Decades of research compiled from the city archives, MPD files, archive and museum collections from as far away as Tuscaloosa, as well as cemeteries, newspapers, and more was gathered and sorted to create a written collection of their history. The first edition was published in 2025, but as the research process in a city like Mobile (which has gone through wars, numerous fires/hurricanes/disasters, and other life-altering events over the past several centuries) is forever ongoing, there will be other editions published as more facts are discovered.

The RESEARCH page (https://carriedalby.com/research/) on my website has a great sampling of local and regional history books. I collect everything from histories of churches to architecture to pictorial accounts that relate to Mobile, Alabama, and her neighbors.

If in-person research is your preference, great places to begin at are the Mobile Public Library's Local History and Genealogy Library, the History Museum of Mobile, and the Minnie Mitchell Archives run by Historic Mobile Preservation Society on the Oakleigh Complex.

About the Author

Carrie Dalby has lived in Mobile, Alabama since 1996, but called locations in both San Diego and Santa Cruz counties home while growing up in California. Serving two terms as president of the Mobile Writers' Guild, five years as the Mobile area Local Liaison for the Society of Children's Book Writers and Illustrators, and helping to coordinate the Mobile Literary Festival are just a few of the writing-related volunteer positions she's held. When Carrie isn't reading, writing, researching, or browsing bookstores, estate sales, or second-hand stores, she can often be found volunteering with the Mobile Citizens Police Academy Alumni Association or attending concerts.

Carrie writes for both teens and adults. *Fortitude* is listed as a "Best Historical Book for Kids" by Grateful American Foundation for its historical accuracy and reader engagement for those in grades fifth through tenth. As of 2026, The Possession Chronicles, The Malevolent Trilogy, and Washington Square Secrets are her Southern Gothic series for adults. She has also published several shorts that can be found in different anthologies as well as her short story collection *Masked Flaws and Other Stories.*

For more information, blog articles, social media links, newsletter sign-up, and more, visit Carrie's website:

carriedalby.com

www.ingramcontent.com/pod-product-compliance
Lightning Source LLC
LaVergne TN
LVHW012110070526
838202LV00056B/5690